God is Ever, Over All Things!

Zabed Mohammad, PhD.
EDUCATOR & RESEARCHER
CANADA

Copyright © 2025 by Zabed Mohammad,
All rights reserved
CANADA.

Library of Congress Cataloging-in-Publication Data
ISBN: 978-1-998923-49-6(Paperback)
ISBN: 978-1-998923-48-9(E-book)

Publisher

Kids Edu Care Inc.
Children's Dedicated Learning Series
Website: www.kidseducare.ca
E-mail: info@kidseducare.ca
Illustration Copyright © 2025 by
Kids Edu Care Inc.
Canada

Design Concept & Illustration
Rakibul Islam Tomal

Zarir and Safwan were best friends who loved to explore together. One sunny day, they discovered a hidden gate at the end of the street.

As Zarir and Safwan roamed around the garden, they heard a soft, gentle voice.

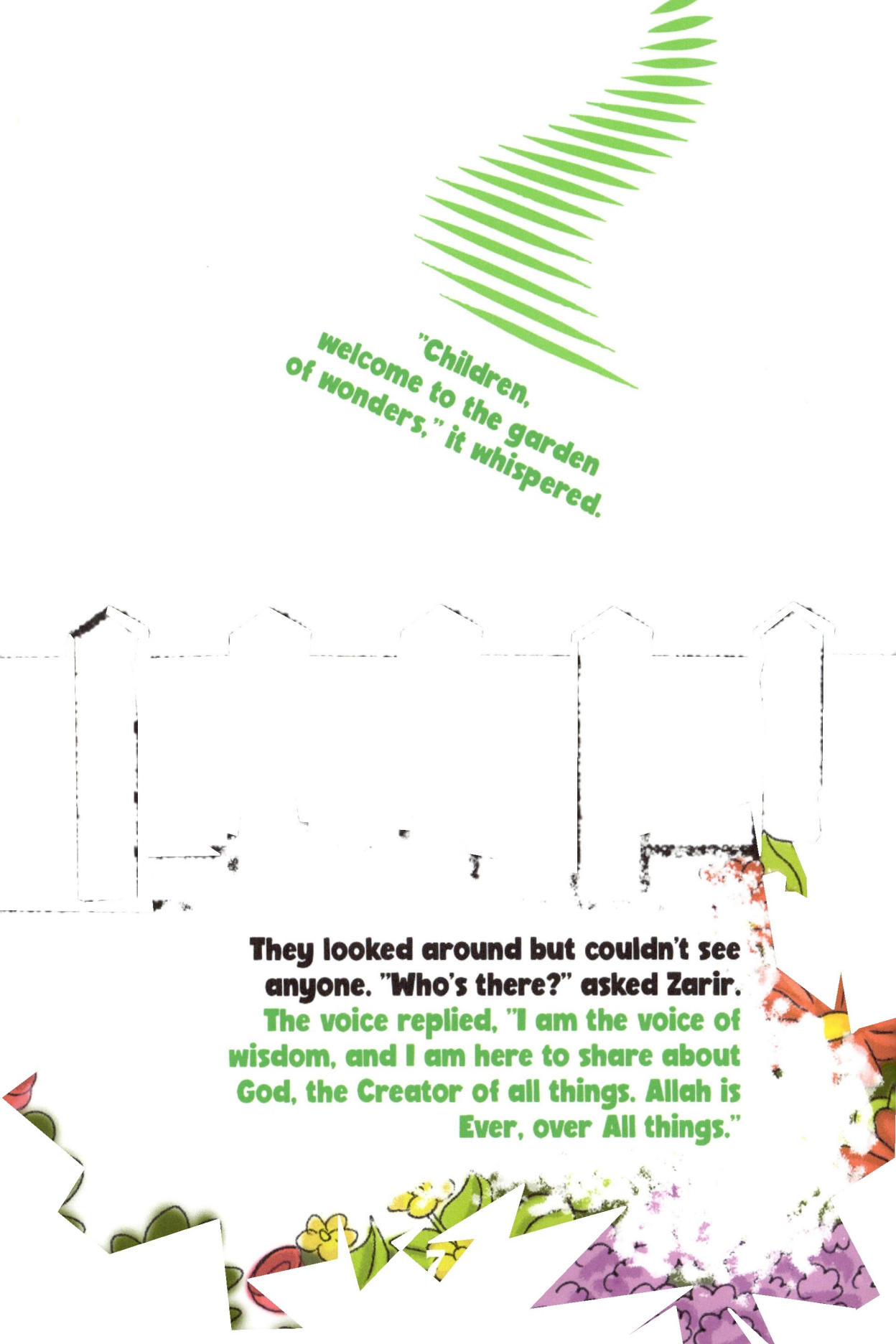

"Children, welcome to the garden of wonders," it whispered.

They looked around but couldn't see anyone. "Who's there?" asked Zarir. The voice replied, "I am the voice of wisdom, and I am here to share about God, the Creator of all things. Allah is Ever, over All things."

As Zarir and Safwan explored the garden, they noticed the beauty and intricacy of the flowers, trees, insects, and animals (Birds, Squirrels, Rabbits).

The voice continued, "Look at the marvelous creations around you. The birds singing, the flowers blooming—they all reflect God's greatness and love for His creation."

Safwan wondered, "Are there any other important teachings about God?"

The voice explained, "Yes, one of the fundamental teachings is the belief in the oneness of God. He is unique, with no partners or equals. It is essential to worship and seek Him

Safwan said, "There are so many things to be thankful for."

The voice nodded, saying, "Indeed, gratitude is an important part of our relationship with God. By expressing gratitude for the blessings in our lives, we

Zarir and Safwan looked at each other and smiled.

The voice continued, "God also blesses us with friendships. Good friends are like treasures; they support and care for each other, just as God cares for all His creation."

Curiosity filled Zarir's eyes as He asked, "How can we learn more about God?"

The voice replied, "God has sent us the Qur'an, a book of guidance and wisdom. It teaches us about God's attributes, His love for us, and how to live a good and fulfilling life."

Zarir wondered, "Sometimes things don't go as planned.

The voice answered, "Life has its ups and downs, which is a beauty and balance of our life. He knows what is best for us, even if we can't always see it. Through patience and reliance on Him, we find peace."

As they walked through the garden, Safwan noticed a butterfly with a torn wing struggling to fly. He gently picked it up and placed it on a flower.

The voice said, "Kindness and compassion towards all creatures are qualities loved by God. Therefore, we should not kill insects or tear flowers or leaves without reason, and we should care for others with love and respect."

Zarir asked, "How can we learn more about God and His creation?"

The voice encouraged them, saying, "Seeking knowledge is a beautiful way to draw closer to God. Explore the wonders of the world, study the sciences, and seek wisdom from the last reveled Holy Book mean Al-Qur'an and the teachings of the Prophet Muhammad (pbuh)."

Zarir and Safwan were eager to memorize the Holy Book Al-Quran, but sometimes things took longer than expected.

The voice shared a valuable lesson, "Patience and trust in God's timing are essential; continue until the finish is the best. Just as a seed needs time to grow into a beautiful tree, our dreams and aspirations require patience, perseverance, and trust in God."

The voice said, "Nature is a reflection of God's beauty and perfection. Take moments to reflect and connect with God through the beauty of His creation. It brings peace and a sense of awe."

Safwan remembered a time when Zarir had accidentally did something wrong. He forgave, and the voice remarked, "Forgiveness and compassion are qualities that please God. Just as you forgave Zarir, God forgives those who sincerely seek His forgiveness and encourages us to forgive others."

Zarir and Safwan met other children in the garden who were also learning about God. They played and laughed together, forming a bond of brotherhood.

Zarir shared his dream
of becoming
a doctor one day.

The voice encouraged her, "Hold on to your dreams and have hope. God can make the impossible possible. With hard work, determination, and trust in God, you can achieve great things."

As they explored further, Zarir and Safwan noticed litter in the garden. They picked it up and threw it in a bin nearby.

As Zarir and Safwan exited, they felt a sense of peace and gratitude.

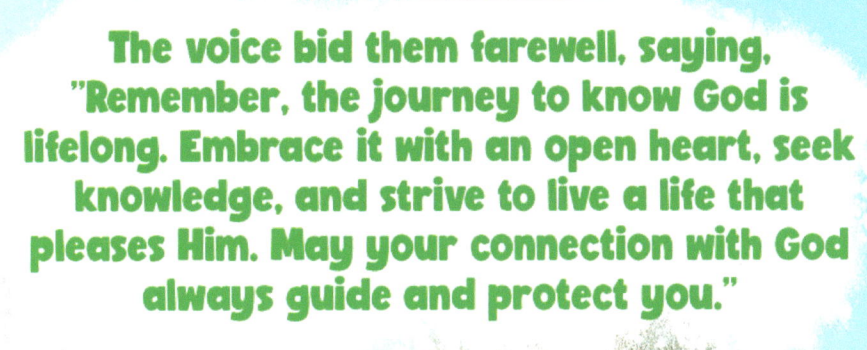

The voice bid them farewell, saying, "Remember, the journey to know God is lifelong. Embrace it with an open heart, seek knowledge, and strive to live a life that pleases Him. May your connection with God always guide and protect you."

www.ingramcontent.com/pod-product-compliance
Lightning Source LLC
LaVergne TN
LVHW072118070426
835510LV00003B/115